I0465085

Historical Mannequin COSTUMES Coloring Book

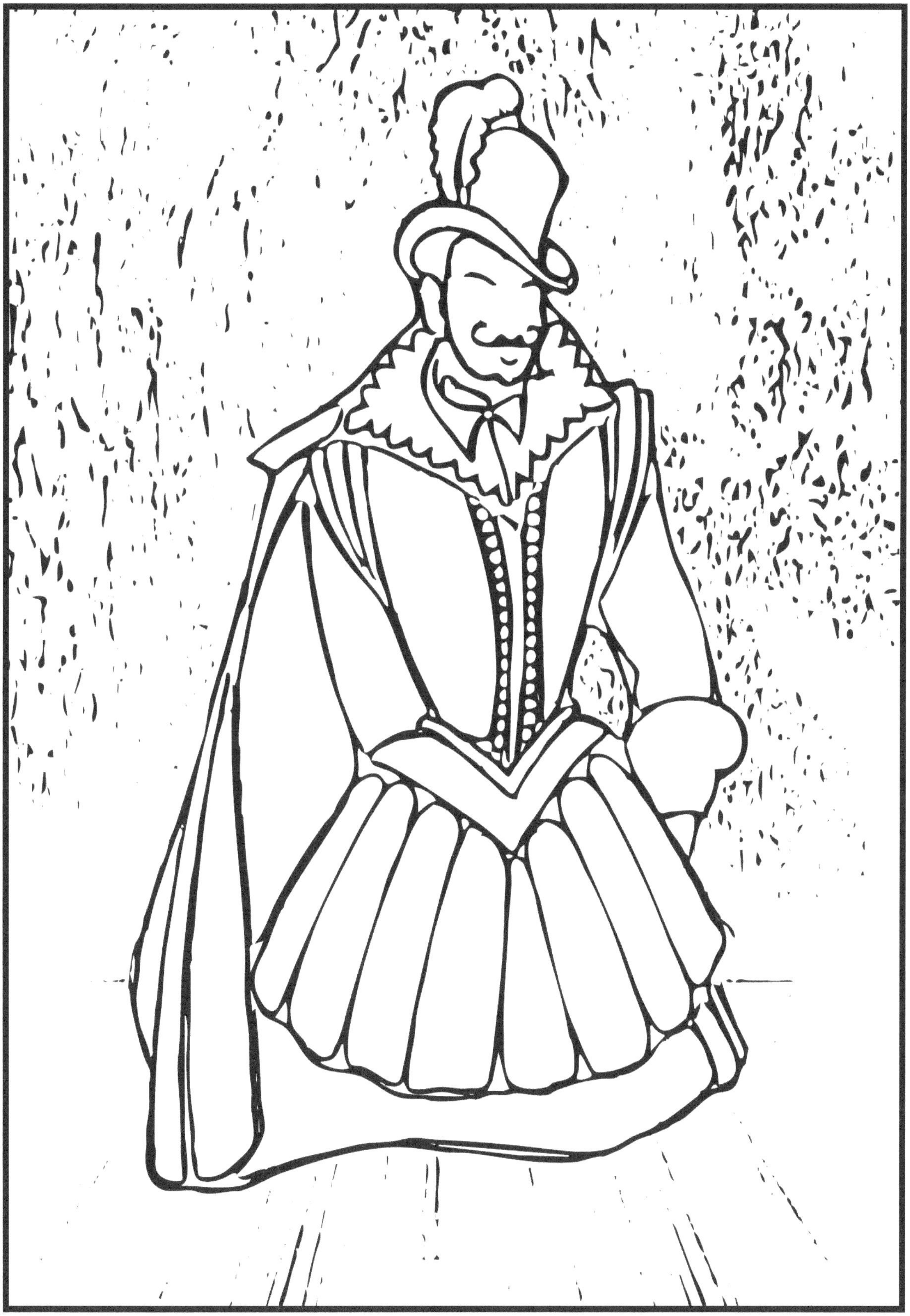

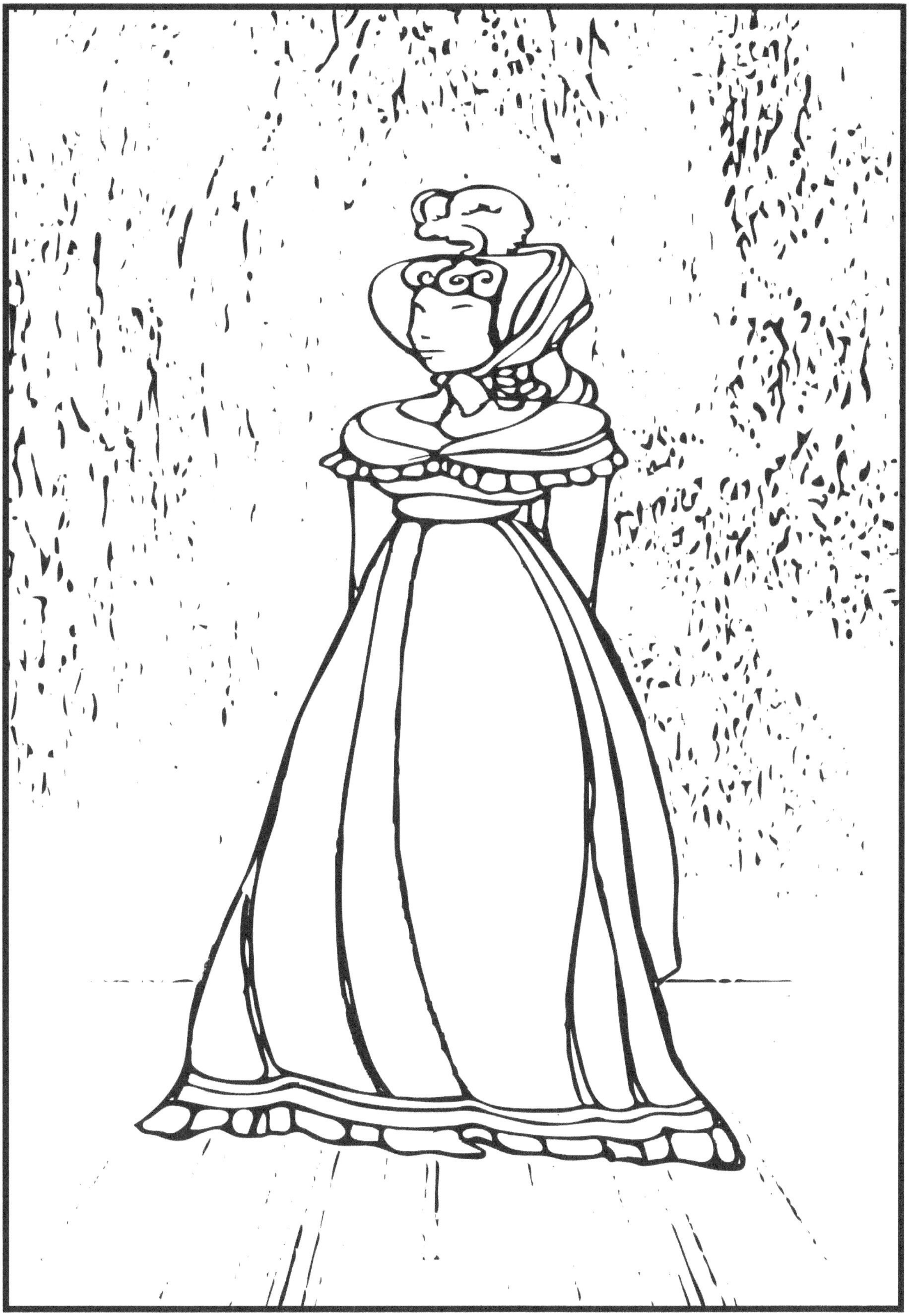

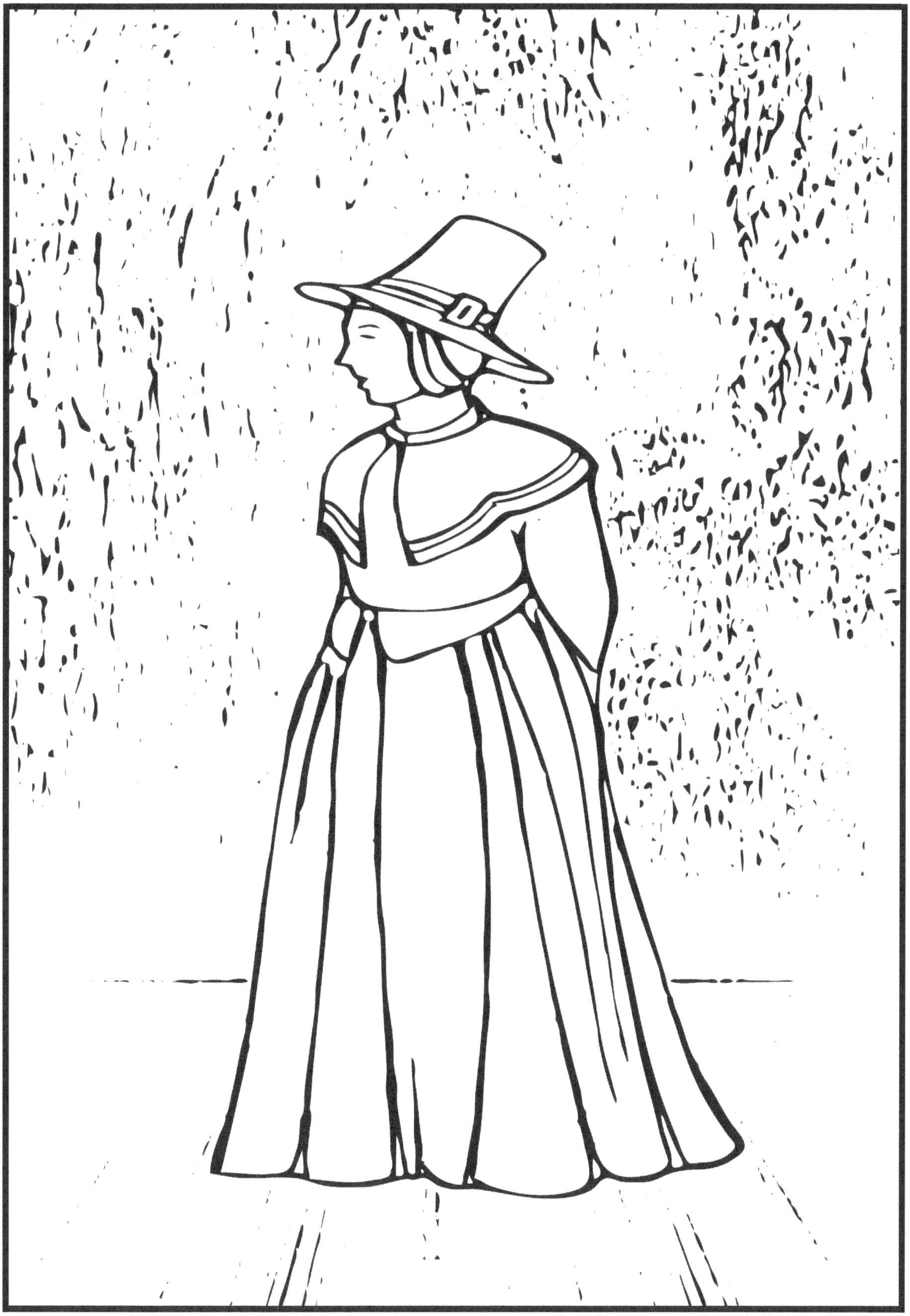

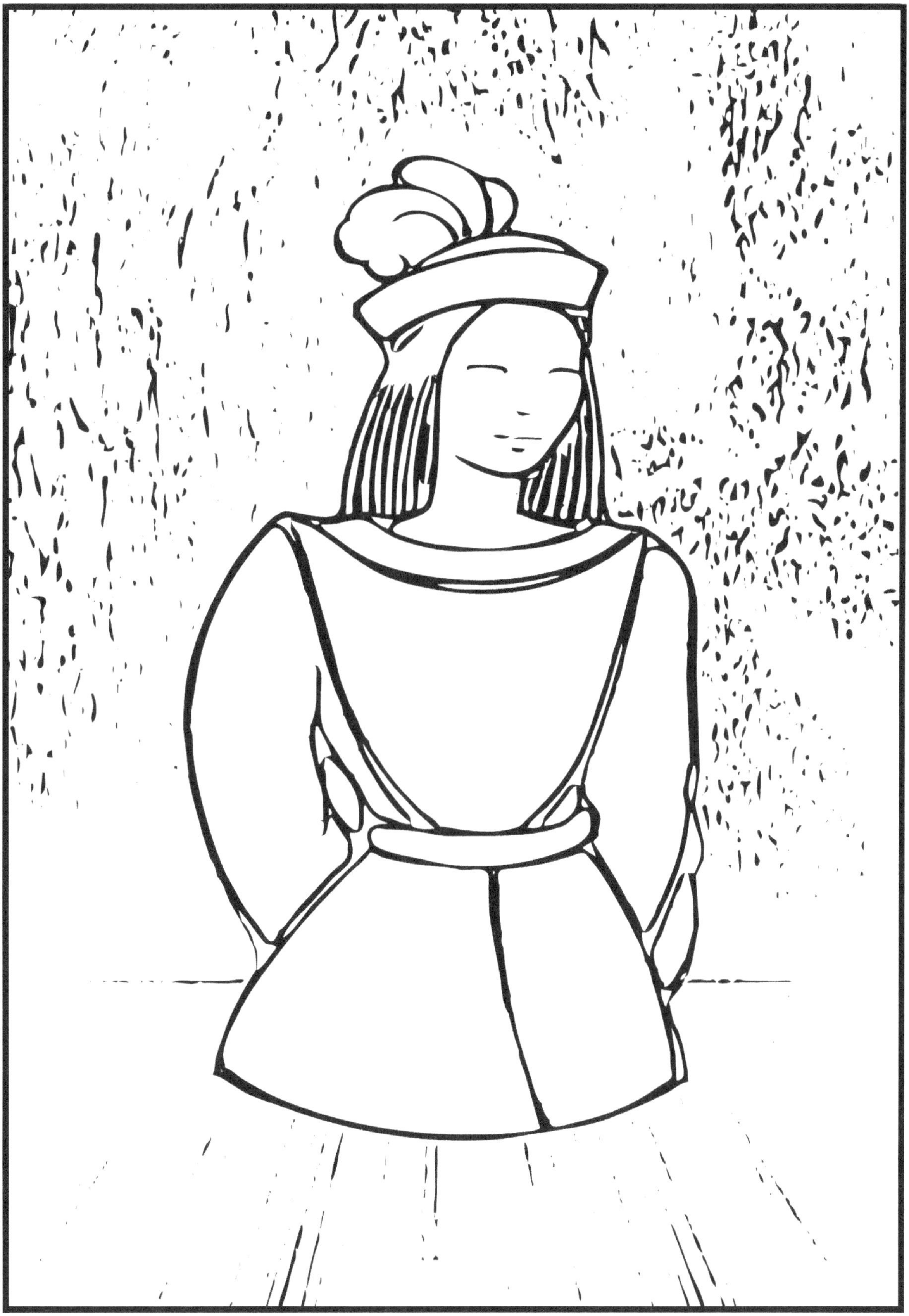

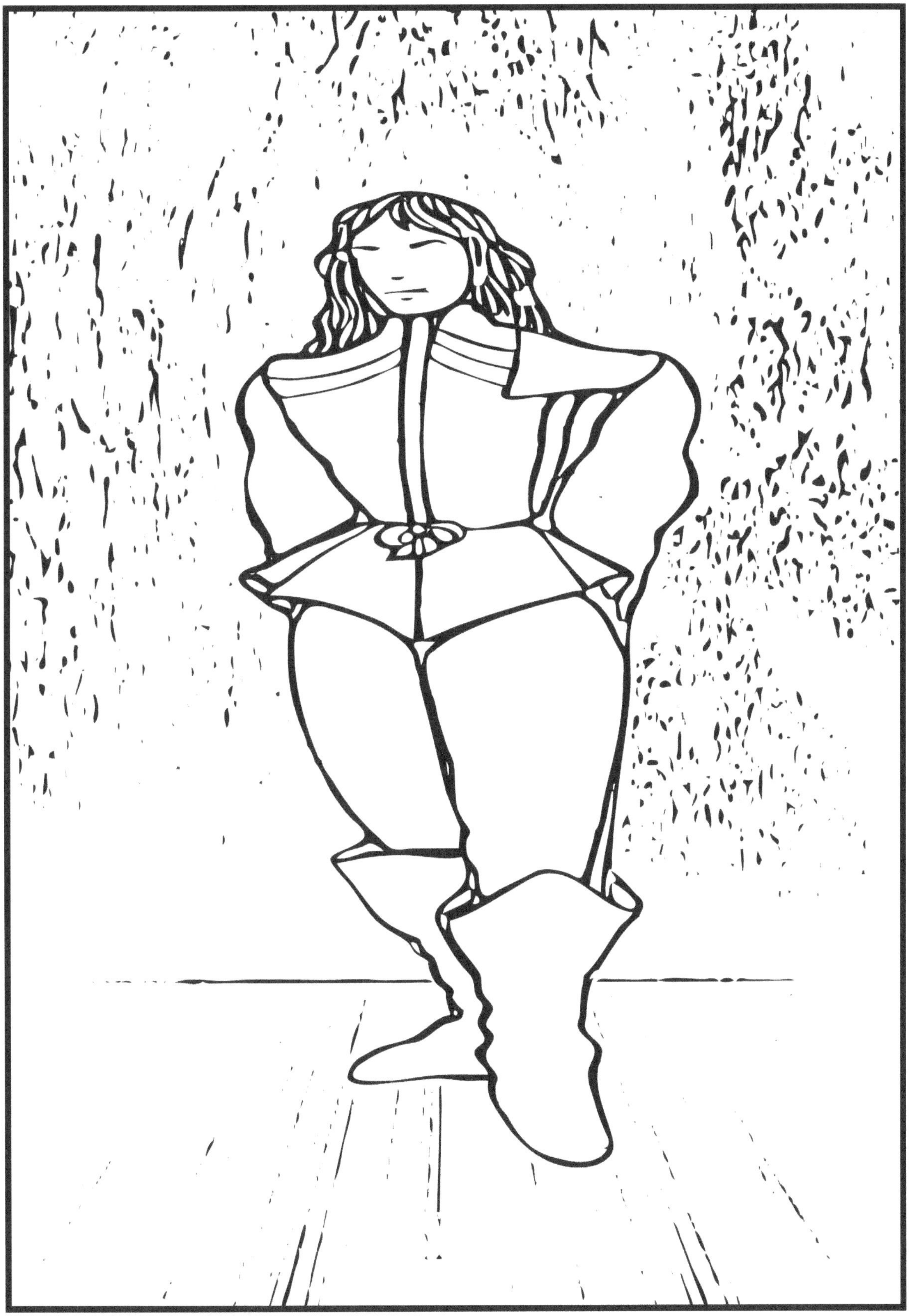

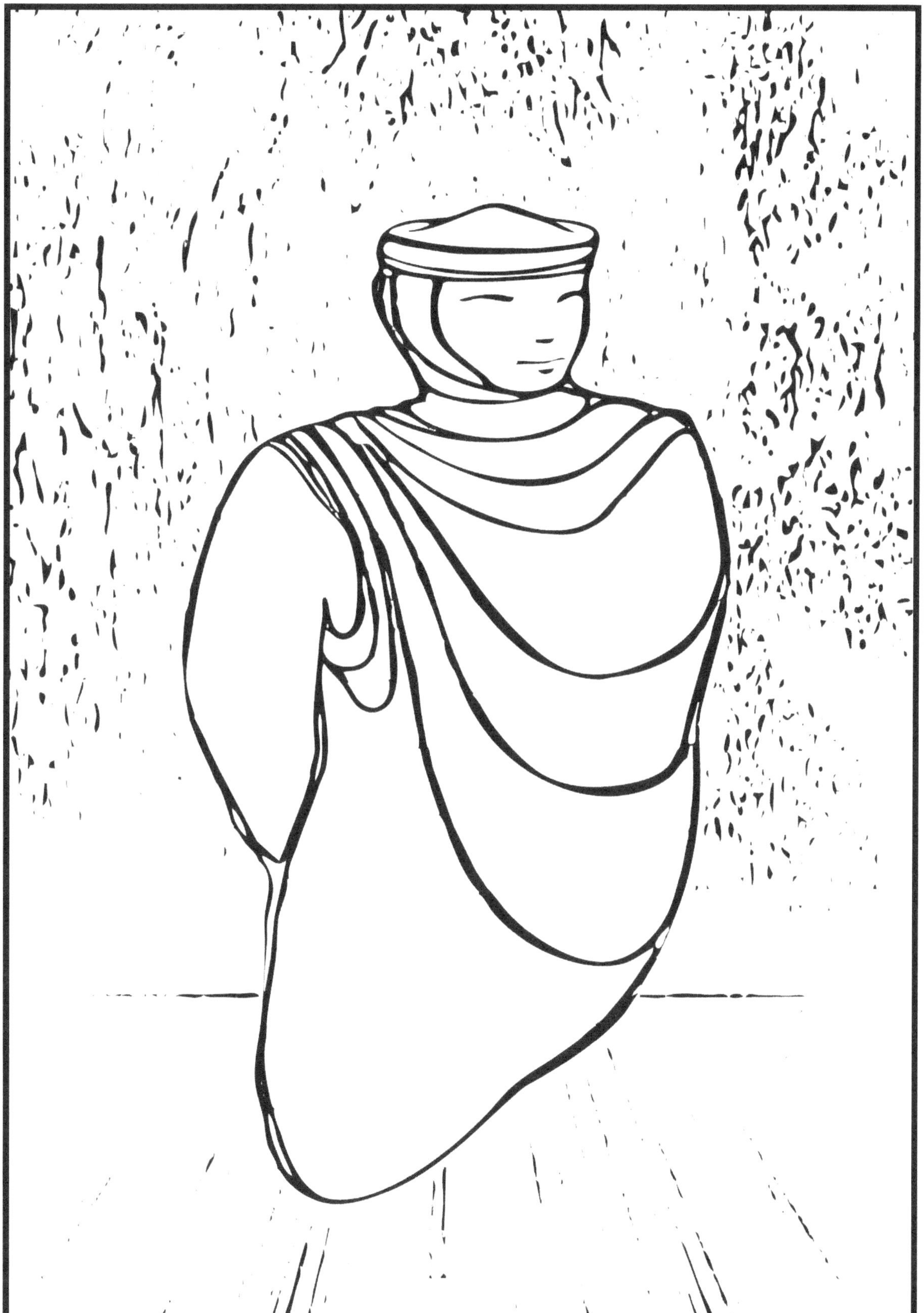

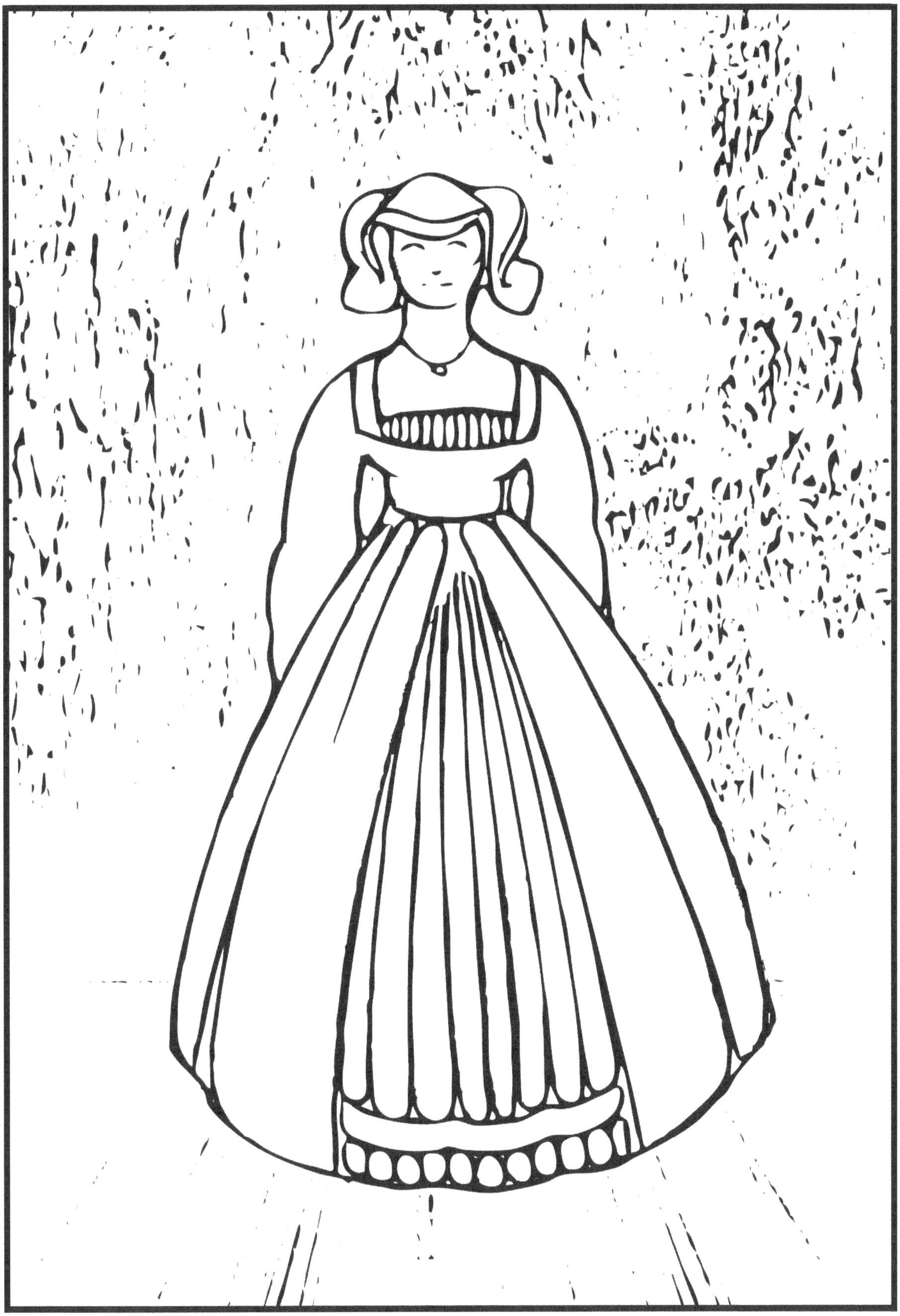

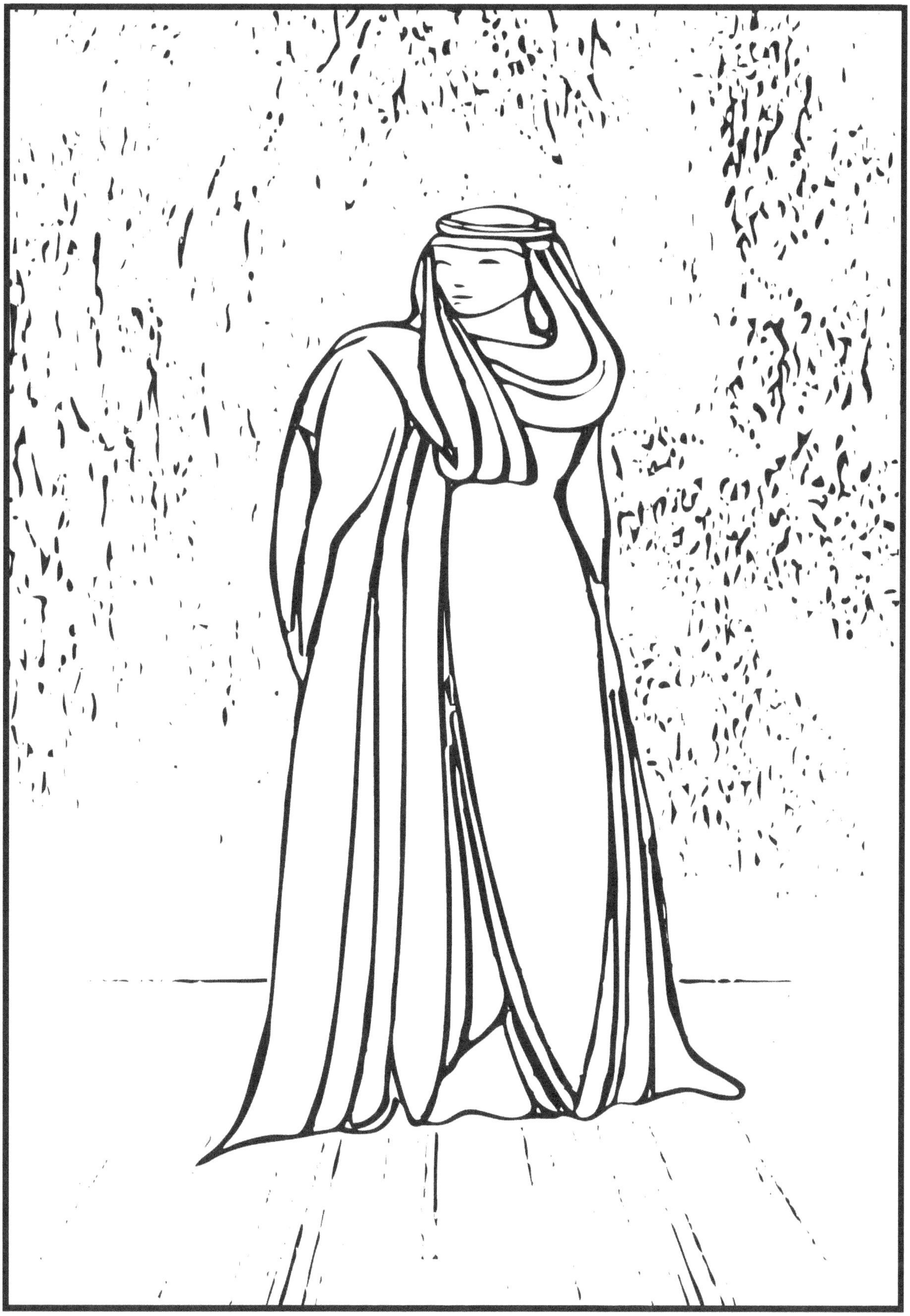

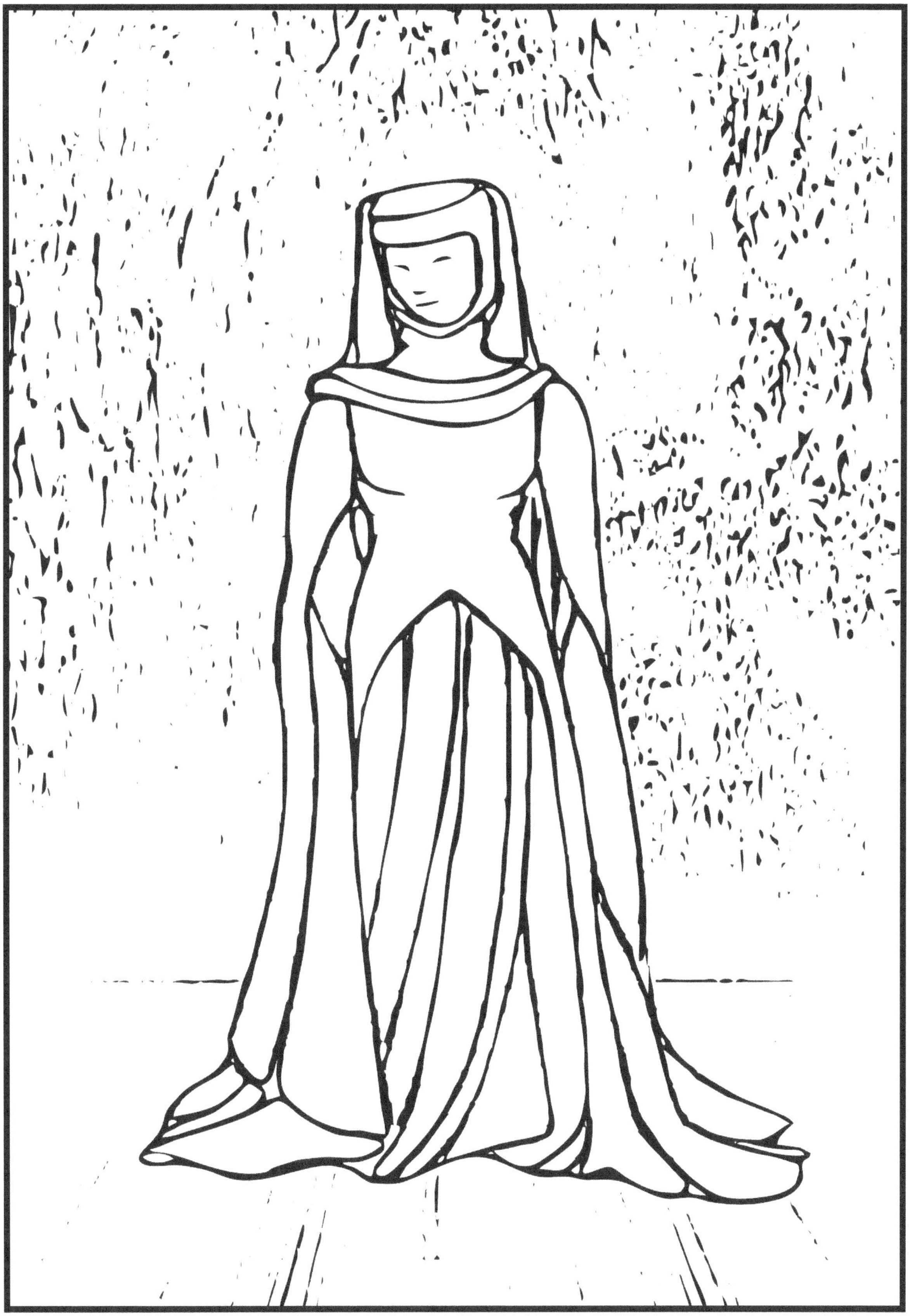

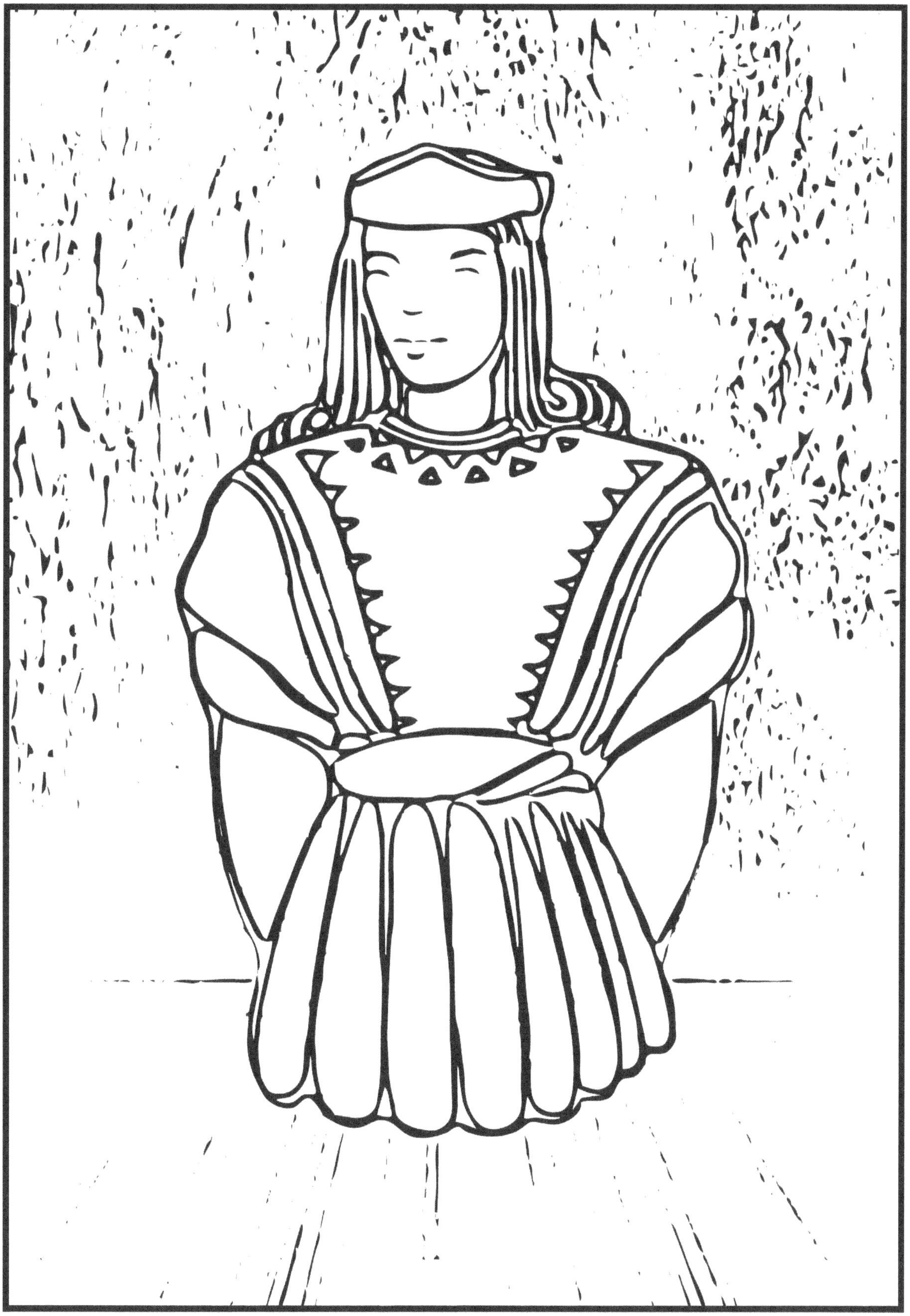

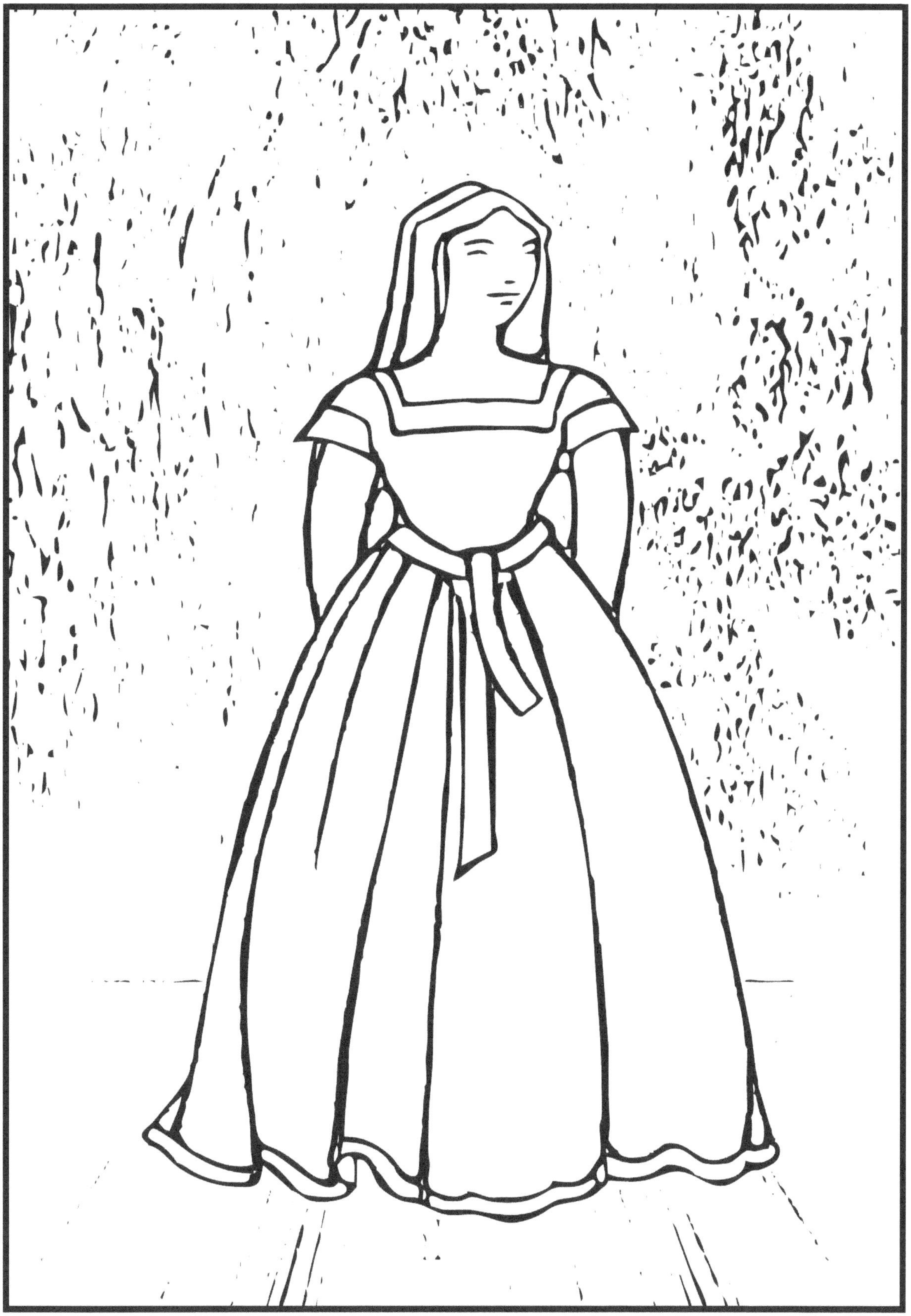

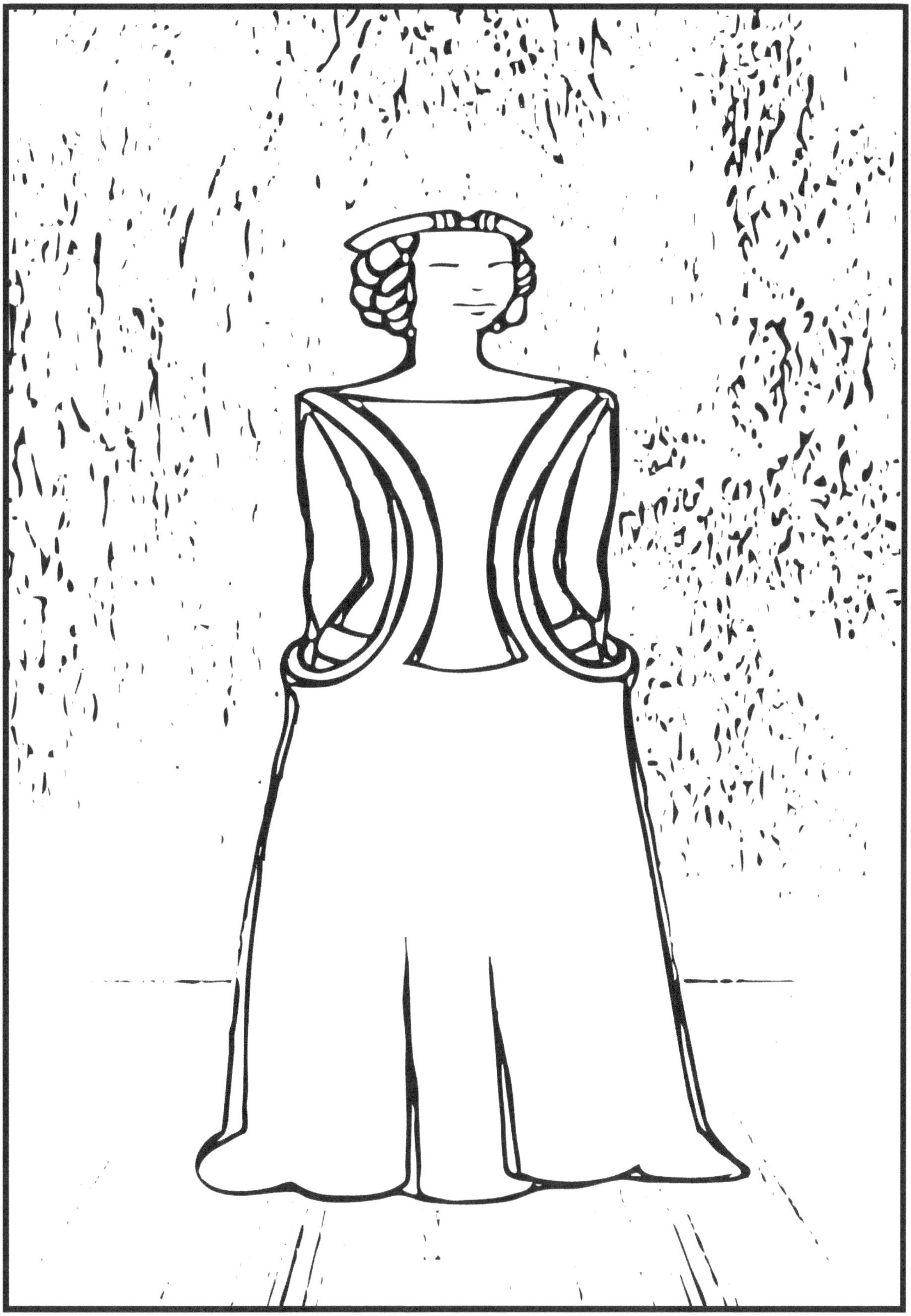

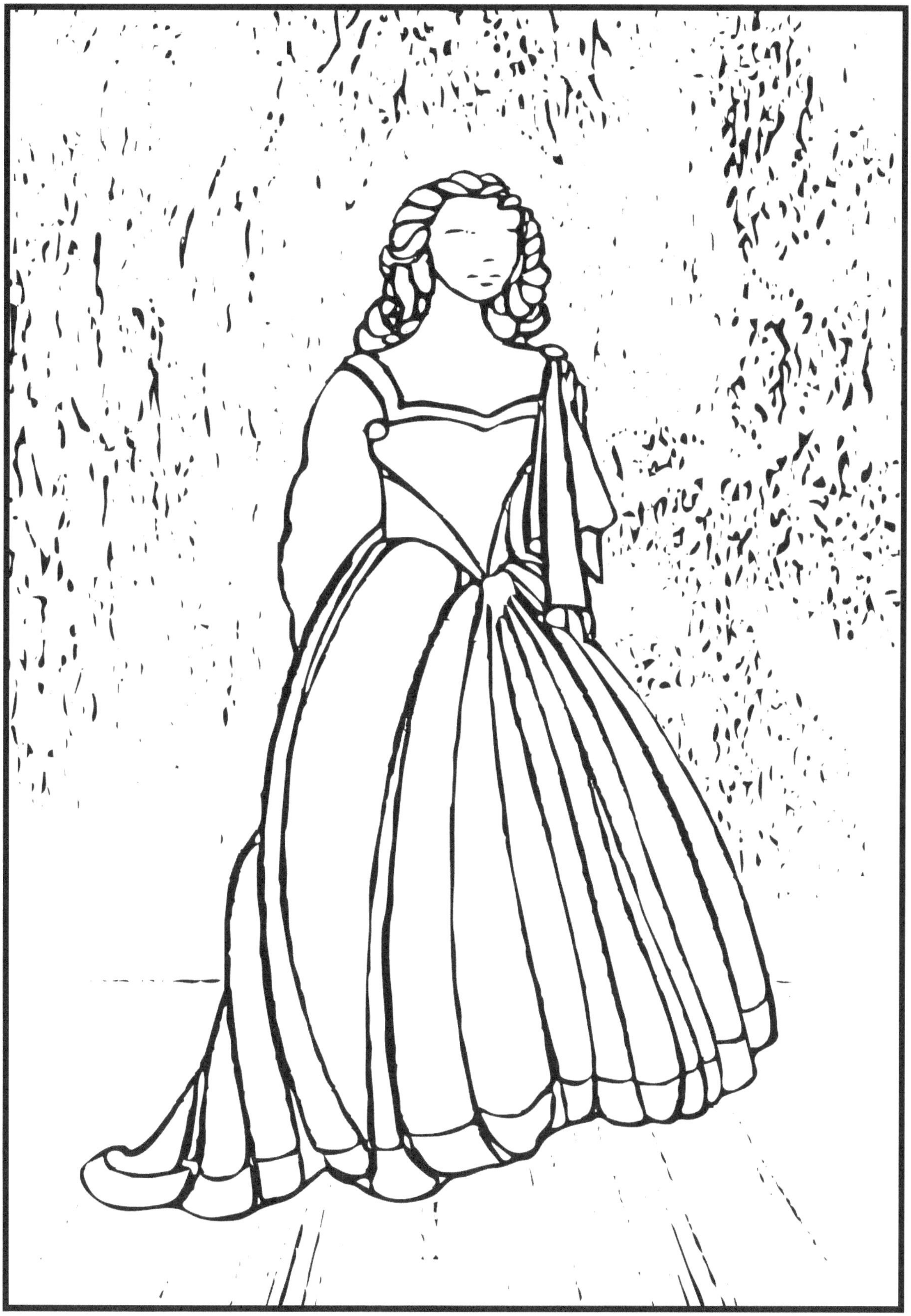

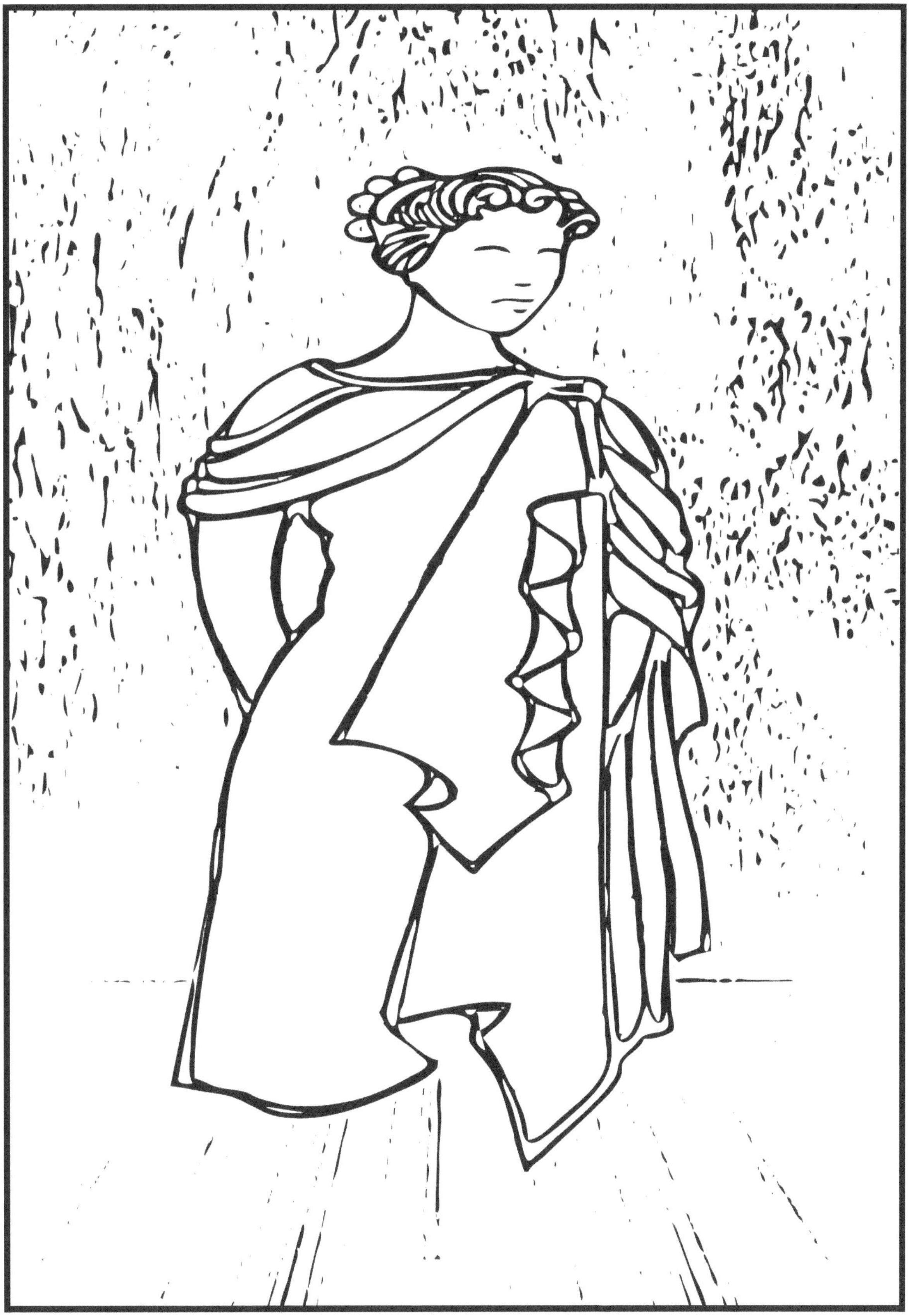

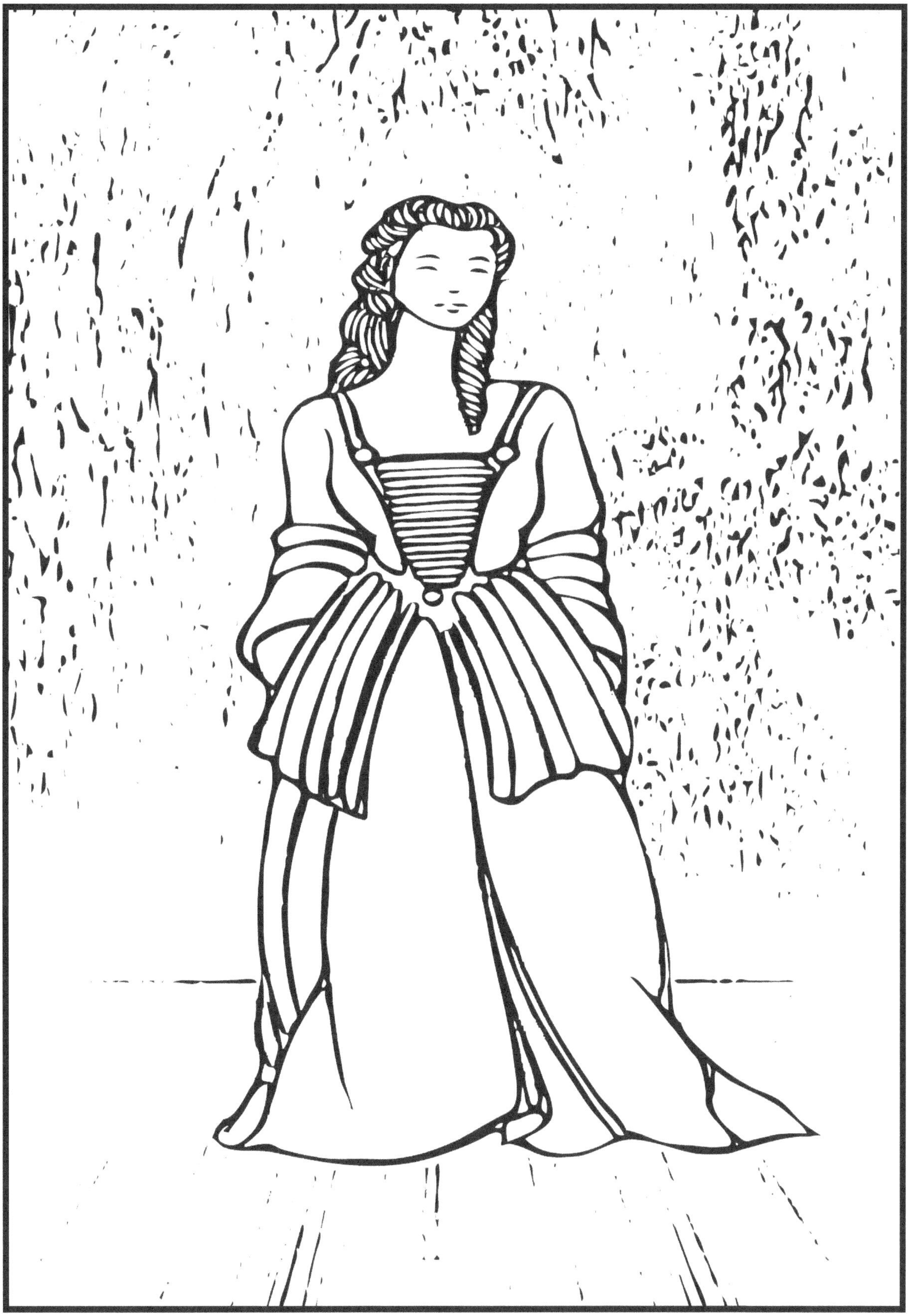

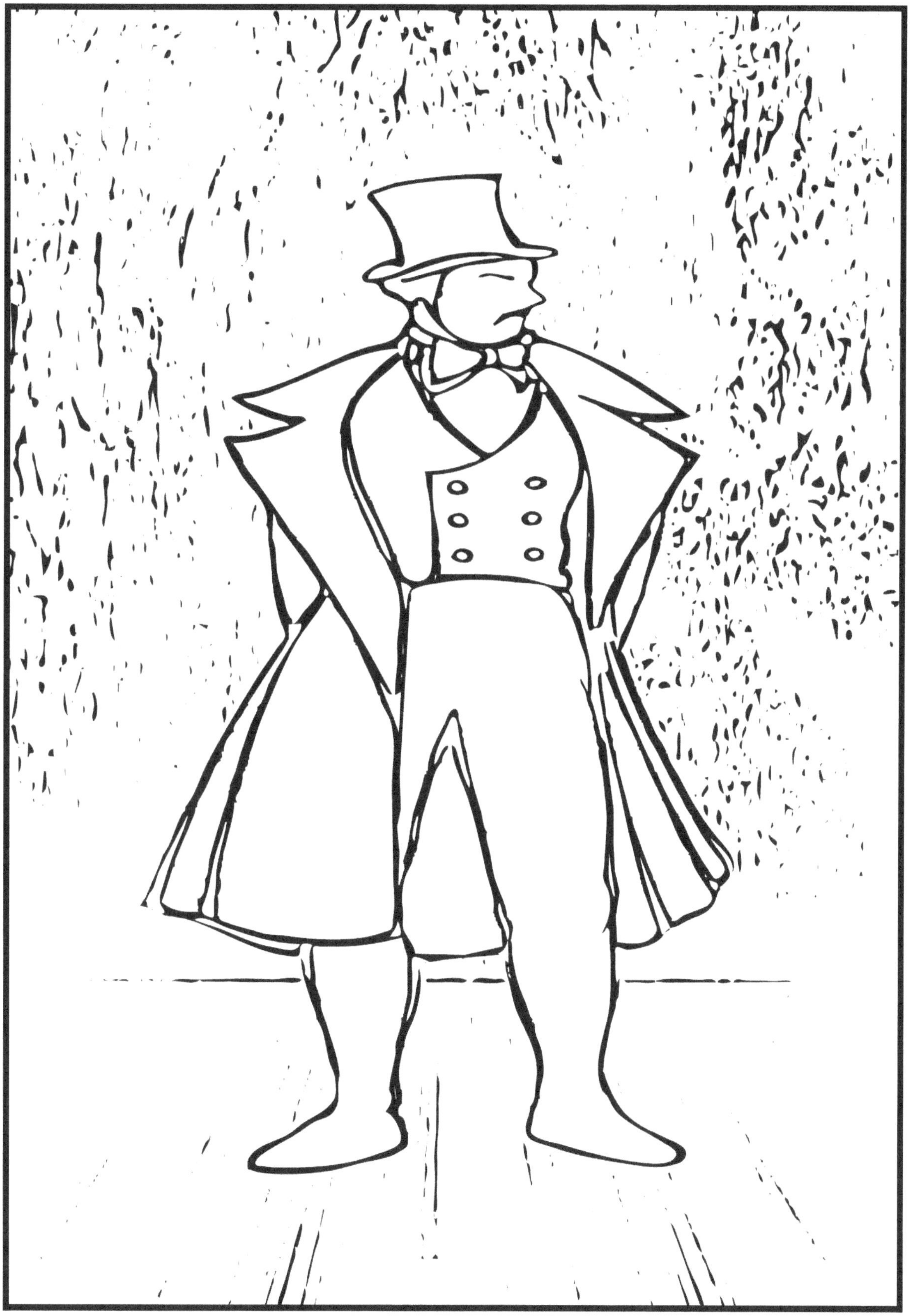

www.ingramcontent.com/pod-product-compliance
Lightning Source LLC
Chambersburg PA
CBHW081313180526
45170CB00007B/2688
9781522901969